Blessed

art for faith's sake series

SERIES EDITORS:
Clayton J. Schmit
J. Frederick Davison

This series of publications is designed to promote the creation of resources for the church at worship. It promotes the creation of two types of material, what we are calling primary and secondary liturgical art.

Like primary liturgical theology, classically understood as the actual prayer and practice of people at worship, primary liturgical art is that which is produced to give voice to God's people in public prayer or private devotion and art that is created as the expression of prayerful people. Secondary art, like secondary theology, is written reflection on material that is created for the sake of the prayer, praise, and meditation of God's people.

The series presents both worship art and theological and pedagogical reflection on the arts of worship. The series title, *Art for Faith's Sake,*ᵗ indicates that, while some art may be created for its own sake, a higher purpose exists for arts that are created for use in prayer and praise.

* *Art for Faith's Sake* is a phrase coined by art collector and church musician, Jerry Evenrud, to whom we are indebted.

Blessed

Monologues for Mary

". . . all generations will call me blessed" Luke 1:48

Jerusha Matsen Neal

FOREWORD BY
Anna Carter Florence

CASCADE *Books* • Eugene, Oregon

BLESSED
Monologues for Mary

Art for Faith's Sake 8

Copyright © 2013 Jerusha Matsen Neal. All rights reserved. Except for brief
quotations in critical publications or reviews, no part of this book may
be reproduced in any manner without prior written permission from the
publisher. Write: Permissions, Wipf and Stock Publishers, 199 W. 8th Ave.,
Suite 3, Eugene, OR 97401.

Cascade Books
An Imprint of Wipf and Stock Publishers
199 W. 8th Ave., Suite 3
Eugene, OR 97401

www.wipfandstock.com

ISBN 13: 978-1-62032-214-7

Allessandro Vittoria Italian, 1525-1608, *The Annunciation*, 1578-1588,
Bronze, 38 ½ x 24 ¼ in. (97.8 x 61.6 cm), Edward E. Ayer Endowment in
memory of Charles L. Hutchinson, 1942.249, The Art Institute of Chicago.
Photography © The Art Institute of Chicago. Used by permission.

Cataloging-in-Publication data:

Neal, Jerusha Matsen

Blessed : monologues for Mary / Jerusha Matsen Neal

xviii + 72 p.; 23 cm

Art for Faith's Sake 8

ISBN 13: 978-1-62032-214-7

1. Monologues. 2. Monologue Sermons. 3. Mary, Blessed Virgin, Saint.
I. Title. II. Series.

BV4307 S7 N35 2013

Manufactured in the USA.

for Wes

Table of Contents

Foreword

In the cathedral of Uppsala in Sweden there is a statue of Mary. She stands in the aisle by the apse, where visitors walk, and is so remarkably lifelike that many do not realize that she is a work of art. Nothing about her is meant to stand out. Her height is only average and her clothes nondescript: blue coat, warm scarf, sensible shoes. If you passed her in the street, you might forget her within moments, or she might remind you of a hundred other women you have met. This is precisely what artist Anders Widoff intended to create: a Mary so ordinary that we might identify with her, mistake her completely, or wonder at her commonplace disguise among us. Yet it is her placement in the cathedral and the title of the work—*Mary (The Return)*—that makes us think twice. Widoff sets her facing the large Vasa Chapel, formerly the Lady Chapel, drawing attention to the fact that after the Reformation, churches in Sweden removed all statues of Mary and renamed her chapels for Swedish kings. Mary all but disappeared from the church. Now she has returned, as both a visitor and a witness. Her intent gaze, looking into the space where she once was, invites us to rethink her place in the Christian story, and in ours.

What you hold in your hand is another work of art, and in this too, Mary returns. She is a chain-smoking single mother, living on the edge. She is a bereft young soldier, raising her dead lover's baby. She is an estranged daughter returning to bury the father she has not seen in years. She is an exhausted pastor of a tired out, all-but-dead congregation. In each of these women, Mary returns to the church, gazing fiercely into a space where she once might have been or may be still—and we, with her. And like the figure of Mary in the Uppsala Cathedral, it isn't so much the breathtaking ordinariness of the women that strikes us as their *placement*, right smack in the middle of our sacred texts and spaces and conversations. Mary in Scripture is one thing; Mary in common life is quite another. It is a peculiarly combustible combination, one that blocks the aisle and interrupts worship. What exactly do they *want*, these women? Are they visitors to our church, who might go away again? Or are they witnesses with a story to tell? And what does any of this have to do with us and our life with God?

Great art always provokes such questions, and with this book Jerusha Matsen Neal has created great art. I do not use the term lightly: these pieces are nothing short of brilliant. Matsen Neal is a superb wordsmith and luminous performer. She writes from a place of deep compassion and uncompromising honesty—a terrifying combination, if as Paul says, the author has no love, and the reader is left to burn and clang alone. But Matsen Neal will never hand us over like that. She has great love: for her characters, for us, for God, and for the church, God's body in this world. It is what gives her portraits of these women such incredible richness. It is what makes us laugh and weep with recognition as their stories unfold. And it is what inspires us to pick up the crumbs of possibility she drops along the way, to follow them and keep following. Everything true the church has ever said, everything beautiful it has ever created, begins with a trail of crumbs and a body broken into great art.

Read these pieces. Put them into the hands of your young people. Let them break open into performances in your sanctuaries and hard conversations in your homes. They are not position statements or lessons in orthodoxy, nor are they puzzles to be solved; that is never the way of art. But they may start something you never knew was ready to begin. They may interpret something you never knew was obscured. They may say something you never knew was true or even yours to say. That is what great art does, and that is the gift Jerusha Matsen Neal has given the church.

What we do next is our gift to God.

Anna Carter Florence
Columbia Theological Seminary
Holy Week, 2012

Preface

In 2008, I received a phone call from a friend who was putting together a conference for women scholars and artists on making space for God in their work. She was specifically drawn to the image of Mary, pregnant with the Word, unable to find space to birth the gift inside her. "So many woman are in this situation," she said. "They have a word to share and are in labor. They are wandering the streets, with no space in their busyness, academic guilds, or religious communities to birth what God has given them." She asked me to tell their stories. My friend did not realize that she had already done something remarkable. She had sketched a line between the person of Mary, popularly remembered for her maternal excellence, submissive silence, and capacity for suffering and the modern female academic. She had connected the experience of writing words on a page and the birth of the Word that is Christ by a female body.

This connection between Mary and words is not new. Medieval scholars often show her reading a book—sometimes in the Bethlehem stable itself![1] Birgitta of Sweden, unique among medieval mystics in that she gave birth to eight children, explicitly connected the experience of Mary's pregnancy to the proclamation of the Word in the

1. See Susan Groag Bell, "Medieval Women Book Owners," in *Sisters and Workers in the Middle Ages*, edited by Judith M. Bennett et al. (Chicago: University of Chicago Press, 1989) 160ff., for a collection of such images.

world.[2] But somewhere in Christian history, either through an emphasis on Mary's passivity or our nervous silence about her generally, this connection between Mary and words—writing, preaching, and pregnancy—was lost.

And the loss was not just a loss for women. To talk about creativity and inspiration—or worse, to talk about the Word of God's entrance into the world—without talking about the bearing bodies of ordinary persons ignores the way that the mystery of grace touches down in human hearts. It ignores the love of God in the grit of life. Through my Protestant eyes, Mary is a woman who is finite and flawed—even as she struggles to be faithful to her calling. And from my perspective as a clergyperson, her struggle seems all too familiar.

Whereas the first set of monologues in this collection deals with the challenges and joys of Christian vocation, I found that I couldn't stop by describing Mary's moment of calling, as if her story ended the moment Christ was born. Similar to my own experience of preaching, Mary does not simply birth the Word; she has to live with it. And living with the Word changes her, frustrates her, and calls her identity into question. The second set of monologues in the book grew out of this disjuncture between ecstasy and disappointment in the work of love. Organized around the question of what constitutes a family—as well as the gospel texts that sketch Mary's story—the collection presses into Mary's feelings of loss and bewilderment as the child she bore distances himself and challenges her. The pieces are not meant to retell her story, but reimagine her questions and protests in light of our modern ambivalence about who we are and to whom we belong.

2. Claire Sahlin, *Birgitta of Sweden and the Voice of Prophesy* (Suffolk: Boyden, 2001) 107.

Metaphors matter. The metaphors we use to talk about theological concepts shape our understanding of what is possible—and theological concepts press us toward metaphor because of all we do not have words to say. Reclaiming the metaphor of Mary's struggle to birth Christ and bear his resemblance as the struggle of the church and its leaders is only part of the picture. Finally, Mary's story invites us to take seriously the complicated questions of the body for theology—or more correctly, it invites us to take seriously the questions of many different bodies who are trying to figure out if and how they are related to the body of Christ. It invites us to have mercy on families that seem like strangers and the strangers that become family, as we wait together for the Spirit's shadow.

How to Use this Book

Space for God and *Promised Land* were written to be separate pieces of theater—though the biblical account of Mary is a common thread throughout. In past performances, music, dance, and visual projections have been used between the monologues to enhance the unity of the whole. The pieces have been performed in secular as well as religious settings. If you would like more information about these past productions, or would like permission to produce the pieces yourself, please contact:

Wipf and Stock Publishers
199 West 8th Avenue, Suite 3
Eugene, OR 97401-2960

Several of these monologues have also been performed as stand-alone pieces in seminary classroom settings, women's retreats, and worship services. I welcome these not-for-profit performances and would be grateful to know how the pieces are finding expression. I have found these smaller readings effective in sparking discussion on vocation, women's stories of faith, ecclesiology, and the relationship between theater and proclamation.

For those who would like to use these monologues as conversation partners in small group bible studies or for private devotions, I have included a list of reflection questions to facilitate the process. These questions are not designed to point the reader toward a single textual meaning—but instead, underscore connections with the biblical witness and make space for diverse testimonies of faith.

Finally, though I did not write these pieces to function as sermons, the monologues may be of interest to those with an eye toward the use of theater as sermonic speech. For those interested in these homiletic concerns, I offer several cautionary reflections as well as some suggestions. As an example of the challenges involved in such hybrid performances and in hope of continued conversation, I conclude this section with one of my own attempts to use drama in a Sunday worship context.

Acknowledgments

Many friends and colleagues have been instrumental in moving this project to completion. Special thanks to Sharon Gartland and InterVarsity Graduate Fellowship, Diversionary Theatre, and Innermission Productions for supporting this work in its early stages—and to the Brehm Center, for its continued commitment to artists of faith. Thank you to Clay Schmidt, Anna Carter Florence, Dan Kirsch, and Scott Erwin who heard small portions of the whole and encouraged me to keep writing. Thank you to Sally A. Brown, Michael Brothers, Richard Lischer, and Charles Campbell for finding a role for these pieces in their seminary teaching. I am especially grateful to Anna Gillette; Wendy Mohler, and Austin Shelley, who brought *Space for God* to life at Princeton Theological Seminary in 2010—and to all those who attended the 2012 reading of *Promised Land*. I am blessed to have a learning community that enriches my writing with insight and Spirit-filled feedback. Over the course of five years, Patricia Loughrey and Annie Dominguez read multiple versions of these pieces with patience and care. I thank them for their careful attention to both the text and my heart.

Most importantly, I thank my family of flesh and families of faith—particularly, Wes, Mercy, and Josiah. You fill our home with milk, honey, and daily joy. You make me brave.

Space for God

Author's Note:

Space for God is a trilogy of monologues commissioned for a women's conference on the relationship between art and faith. Women scholars, scientists, and artists gathered for a weekend retreat on making creative space for God in their lives and in the world. The final piece, the most sermon-like, was performed as part of the closing worship service.

These modern parables on the nature of our calling as women—and as human beings—use the biblical story of Mary as a conversation partner. In Christian tradition, Mary is the mother of the Word—a title derived from Christ's designation as the Word of God (John 1:1). The pieces take this title seriously—reinterpreting Mary's story to refer, not only to the experience of childbirth and mothering, but also to the very real labor of creative, scientific, word-driven work. What does Mary's choice to make space for the Word in her body—and her literal struggle to find space to give birth in the crowded streets of Bethlehem—have to teach women who are pregnant with creative life? Women who face resistance and closed doors from their communities? Women who deal with that pain by filling their lives with busyness, rather than the work they know they were born to do?

Space for God is finally about the cost and joy of living into that calling. Medieval paintings often depict Mary as either reading a book or spinning thread when approached by the angel Gabriel. The thread that ties her words and witness to our own lies at the heart of this project.

Allessandro Vittoria Italian, 1525–1608, *The Annunciation*,
1578–1588, Bronze, 38 ½ x 24 ¼ in. (97.8 x 61.6 cm), Edward E.
Ayer Endowment in memory of Charles L. Hutchinson, 1942.249,
The Art Institute of Chicago.
Photography © The Art Institute of Chicago.

The Annunciation

*"Do not be afraid, Mary. You have found
favor with God." Luke 1:30*

(A woman sits on a museum bench, facing the audience. Behind her is projected an image of Alessandro Vittoria's bronze relief, The Annunciation. *She is dressed in an urban style, an art museum tote bag at her feet. She is knitting—quite fixedly. Her project is currently indeterminate and scarlet red. She looks up and attempts a joke.)*

Be careful. Knitting needles are dangerous weapons, I'm told.

(She laughs—then clears her throat.)

I shouldn't joke. It could be like the airport. I'm not supposed to have these in here. Museum policy. But don't tell. Artie over there could get in trouble. *(Conspiratorially.)* I was lucky to find a museum guard who looks the other way. He has a knitting mother. He knows the compulsion a good worsted weight yarn in a stockinette stitch can have on a woman. Lets me do my thing. As long as I can sneak the needles in, I'm good to go.

(She nods in the direction of the audience, as if she is facing Vittoria's bronze.)

Knitting away with the Virgin Mary . . . Mother of the divine Word. A graduate student stuck in chapter three of a five chapter dissertation will try almost anything.

(She smiles stiffly, continuing to knit as she speaks.)

Do you knit? Most people knit to relax. I do guilt knitting. Something to keep my hands busy while I'm hiding out. You don't run into members of your committee at the Art Institute nearly as often as at the university library. And the knitting itself is quite reassuring . . . lots of repetition and forgiveness. You make a mistake, it unravels beautifully. You just . . . *(pantomimes pulling out a row with a trill of the tongue)* . . . pull it out. Untangling anything should be that easy. I like pulling out the stitches more than I like making them. It's the historian in me. Unraveling patterns to find the—*(self-importantly)* single causal thread. *(A sheepish smile.)* Who'm I kidding? Unraveling the stitches means I'm not lugging around a seventeen-foot scarf that gives my procrastination away. I've been knitting ever since I stopped writing.

(Gestures again toward the bronze.)

I saw this bronze about then too. I couldn't get it out of my head.

Annunciation paintings are a dime a dozen in this place, but this one's different.

She's scared, isn't she? I never pictured her scared before. She looks like she's ready to bolt. I suppose that makes sense. She's got a tough row to hoe. But there are worse things. Like never giving birth to any word worth anything—much less a Word to change the world. Most women don't get annunciations in the middle of the night telling them they're "highly favored" or solving the "seminal quandary" Dr. Landau posed in their proposal review. I'd like an angel Gabriel for that—thank you very much.

Jay thinks I'm working. He kisses me goodbye every morning—thinks I'm off to do footnote-collecting or page-formatting or spell-checking or whatever it is he thinks I do. I give him some story over dinner, and he always says the same thing, "One day closer to be done, babe." One day closer to being done.

Some days I'm scared it's going to get done, and it won't be worth the trees I killed to write it. You know, not all of us are Marys. Some of us are just ordinary girls with greater than average intellect and a generally good work ethic. When we're not hiding out and knitting.

(She sees Artie offstage, nods in his direction, and quickly puts knitting in bag; in explanation,)

We have a signal.

(Standing, she walks behind the bench, attempting to look casual. She is uncomfortable with her hands unoccupied.)

I guess I think if I sit here long enough and put in my time, Mother Mary will tell me her secret . . . how she got picked. How I can get picked too.

Trust me, I wouldn't be here if I didn't think it would help. Museums freak me out. Too much space . . . too much white on the walls. Like a glowing white computer screen waiting for words.

(Examining picture again, a memory calms her.)

But then, there is that bronze . . . the wind whipping Mary's veil. I can almost feel that wind—like afternoon storms when I was a girl. My dad spent his summers in Indonesia. He was a textile artist. I used to fall asleep under cloths he had painted by hand—the rain pounding the roof. He knew something about inspiration—my dad—about Spirit bigger than you that fills you up with color and life . . . and makes a difference. He always said he wanted to paint canvases that people could run between their fingers, cloths that wrapped babies, and covered marriage beds. Cloths that draped a memory.

(Looks in Artie's direction again and takes out knitting.)

Coast is clear.

My dad's why I'm a historian in the first place. I'm not an artist. But, he taught me the importance of everyday things, everyday events. My dad loved the weave of a cloth—the part that every thread would play. I thought that's what studying history would mean—giving every thread its due.

But now I'm somewhere in the middle of my tome on "Emergent Nationalism and Labor Movements in Sumatran Palm Plantations, 1913–1947"—*(self-deprecating aside)* ya' want to read it already don't you?—and I wonder. I wonder if all these words and all this work matter nearly as much as I want them too. I never see the whole cloth anymore —just threads—and lately, even those slip in and out of focus.

The knitting helps. It reminds me what a single thread can do.

(She looks at yarn in her hands.)

And what it can't.

I taught myself to knit seven months ago. I'm still not very good. I always get my stitches too tight—but I thought I could at least make something warm to wrap up a baby on cold nights. Something a child could remember as she grew. Jay and I'd been trying for two years. And then it came . . . my own Annunciation. My own personal Gabriel, in the form of two little lines on a plastic stick.

But not all of us are Marys.

No fall or trauma. No warning. Just some cramping and a thread of blood that didn't stop for days. And even though there was no more baby to knit for, I couldn't put the needles away. To see them sitting unused was just one more reminder that God hadn't send an angel for me.

(After a pause.) They have these shadow puppet plays in Yogya. A puppeteer creates these epics by casting shadows on a lighted screen. The performance goes on all night. And my dad and I used to argue about what side of the

screen to sit on—because you could sit on either. You could watch the puppeteer himself, from the backside of the screen, moving three or four puppets at a time . . . or you could sit in front and watch the illusion—the shadows coming to life. My dad always wanted the illusion, of course. I wanted to see the man behind the screen. I wanted to see the man making the shadows.

And I still do. I want to see this God whose shadows are supposed to be dancing across my life, because I think He's left the building. "The Holy Spirit will overshadow you," Gabriel says to Mary. I got no such promise from my Puppeteer.

I showed up, and God didn't. My body doesn't do what it's supposed to do . . . my words have all been said before. I have nothing of interest to say. Nothing shiny and brilliant and full of wind and color. All I have is me and silent, empty spaces, and I'm not to blame. I put in the time. That angel *(indicates the picture)* never came for me.

(Angry now.) I don't want to write anymore if my work is just another miscarriage waiting to happen, if it was never meant to come to term. Maybe some women are meant to have annunciations and some aren't. Some women have words that fall to them fully formed like babies from heaven . . . and some spend their lives writing summaries of words already written.

(The anguished secret comes.)

Jay says we'll try again after the dissertation's finished.

And so I toss the train stubs from my daily ride downtown—so he won't know I'm playing hooky. I pay the museum admission fee with cash, like this is some great, sad, unfaithfulness. Which I suppose it is.

And I sit here with the only Mary I've seen smart enough to be scared of a God who doesn't let you keep the babies you conceive . . . or even the babies you bear. A Mary, who knows the danger of saying, "Let it be with me accord-ing to your word" but says it anyway—babies fluttering all around her, cluttering the sky. No halos or stillness, just a storm—and an angel who shows up shouting his "Hail Mary" over the wind, *(with indignation)* telling her to not to be afraid.

(Speaking to the angel in the painting, as if he is in front of her.)

Do you even know what it'll cost to try again? To make space in my life for words and joy and the emptiness that comes every month when another scarlet thread means we unravel our hopes and start from the beginning. Do you know what it will cost to lay down this *(indicates the knit-ting)* work of my hands so something new can come? To lay aside this cloth that drapes *my* memory?

(As she faces the picture, her face changes—a dawning insight. She gathers her composure and speaks very simply.)

I know why Mary's afraid. It's not that the angel isn't coming. It's that he's already here . . . right here in this quiet space . . . waiting for an answer.

(She becomes very still, her knitting resting on her lap.)

In Greek mythology, there were three Fates who wove the fabric of the world. And every time they cut a thread, somebody died. That's the joy of knitting. No scissors in-volved. Nothing ever gets cut . . . and it never has to be finished, so long as you keep at it. Especially if you keep pulling out your stitches. It's a much less dangerous pas-time. No matter what museum policy says.

Endings are hard. Which means that sometimes be-ginnings are harder.

(She gathers courage and slowly, with sacred tenderness, she takes scissors from her bag and cuts the thread connecting the ball of yarn to her work.)

"Let it be with me . . ."

(She gently wraps her work around her needles and puts them away. With a breath, she stands and exits the gallery, leaving behind a scarlet ball of yarn.)

The Call

"She laid him in a manger, because there was no room for them in the inn." Luke 2:7b

(A woman stands in bathrobe and slippers, surrounded by things you might find in a garage: a lawnmower, boxes of decorations, portable shelves cluttered with garden tools. Behind her stands a pulpit, draped with a sheet.)

I was driving home from the Chick 'n Pig meat locker when I seen it. A sign from God. Just sittin' there plain as the baby Jesus in the manger. 'Cept 'stead of a stable, I was passing the Grundy's fallin-down mess of a house. And there it was. Sometimes signs from God are like that. They call to ya' from the back of a picked-over yard sale. Even 'fore I pulled up that dirt driveway, I was already figurin' how to fit it in my car. It looked so forlorn sitting 'tween the cowboy boot lamp and the Coca-Cola lawn chair. Brought tears to my eyes. Miss Grundy said her late husband used to teach the Brady Volunteer Firefighter classes standing behind it. Said a real-live podium made the boys pay attention, made 'em show some respect. But this weren't no podium.

This was a pulpit . . . in-cog-ni-to.

(She stretches out the word, smiling—as if she loves the feel of it on her tongue.)

Ran my hand over the wood. Corners, banged up. Finish, all but gone. No cross on the front, but there's no doubt what it was. Things know what they are, and if you listen, they tell you. There was deep water in that wood, water that had laid still too long waitin' to run. There was blood too. Gave me a mean splinter in half-a-minute. That's 'at made me certain sure. A podium might be made of wood. But a pulpit's made of water and blood. It's a livin' thing. And here it was, set out in the August sun in the middle of a crabgrass patch. I didn't know where I'd put it . . . or what I'd do with it. But you can't much argue with a sign from God. Specially one that don't cost you but $5. That pulpit was mine.

People are funny about divine signs. They's a bit embarrassed by 'em. Sorta like you might feel 'bout what my mama called "mole-tunnels" in a cake.

(She begins opening two lawn chairs.)

You know what I mean. Ya' make a red velvet masterpiece and cut it open to find air pockets windin' all through. The ladies know it's your fault too, even if they don't say so. Ya' got to whipping that batter, made yer air bubbles big as quarters, and forgot to drop the pan on the counter to pop 'em.

(She firmly taps a chair on the ground to demonstrate.)

My mama used to say mole tunnels showed an over-zealous enthusiasm and a wanderin' mind.

Signs from God is the same way, when you been a Missionary Baptist since the day you were born. That's different from a Free-Will Baptist or a Primitive Baptist or a Fundamental, Independent, Dispensational Baptist for all you in the rest of the world who just thought we were Southern. Missionary Baptists believe in the Word with no frilly decoration. We feel it in the soles of our non-dancing feet . . . the solid weight of the Holy Script holding us up and rooting us down. In my church, you can't have any signs from God too big or people gonna tell you you've been mixing your batter more than you should . . . and you're liable to get dropped.

(She picks up a small wood memory box and cradles it as she speaks.)

But signs don't go away just by saying they ain't so. They're not like a billboard that you can paint over or block out with the blink of an eye. They're like a call. A bird call from a bird you hope is singing for you. You can't shut yer ears, even when yer palms is pressed against your head. The song just sneaks inside. You can't unhear it once it's gotten in. It's a part of you—like that bug that crawled into Uncle Walter's ear and died. We tried to scrape it out . . . flush it out . . . but the best we could do was crush it down until it left its blood behind inside him. A sign from God is the same. It may stop buzzin' in your ear, but it leaves a stain.

'Course that don't mean you tell anybody about it. There are things you fess up to in this world and there are things better left . . . incognito. It don't take you long to figure out which is which.

When I was a little girl, I received a sign.

(She sits in a lawn chair, and pulls a bird feather from the memory box.)

I was swimming with my brothers in the quarry swimming hole, swinging out on a rope over deep water and dropping like a stone. I swung out, and a bird flew from my left and hit my cheek in midair. Just like it were aiming. I felt its smooth breast hot on my face, its claws grazin' my chin. Its feathers brushed my lips. And then *(dropping the feather back inside the box),* I fell into green water. I opened my eyes and saw round bubbles rising toward the sun like angels going to heaven. Climbing Jacob's ladder. And I knew . . . Just like Jesus knew when the dove descended. Like Isaiah knew in that cherubim-filled temple. My mouth

had been made holy. My mouth had been called to preach.
I stayed under that water 'til my lungs were burning up . . .
the silence flooding my ears. Because I knew I'd had a call .
. . and I knew that I could never tell a soul.

(She rouses herself and stands with energy.)

Everybody knows a woman can't preach. It's as true as
any black and white Bible verse you want to pick—as sure as
the brick of the Brady Baptist meeting hall. Unchangin' as
my mama's calloused knees, red from praying or weeding,
one.

(Suddenly still.)

But all the same, things know what they are. And I
was a preacher. I just musta been born wrong. I couldna'
help wonderin' why God'd make a preacher in the shape of
woman who could never stand and do the deed. It didn't
make no sense. 'Cause somethin' happens to a calling you
squirrel away. It goes underground and, like a ghost in a
cellar, it don't leave you alone.

*(She pulls a blue ribbon from the box and fingers it
throughout this next memory.)*

I had a girlfriend growing up named Jeremiah June.
Strange name, I know. I think her mama wanted a boy. Her
people came from the House of Prayer with Signs Following
Church down by the river. We didn't associate with House
of Prayer folk. They were backward and dirty and they
handled snakes at their weekend services. My mama would
not abide religious fanaticism of that sort. But Jeremiah and
I were friends anyway—on the sly. One night, Miah told me
afterward, a man had handed one of those snakes to her.
Children don't usually do the handling, but Miah said that
night the anointing was there. She said it felt like cool death
and squirming life wrapping you up in one. Like fear and
dizzy joy at just being alive . . . just being brave enough to do
the deed. She could never leave the snakes alone after that.

I used to help her find 'em down by the river. One Sunday, she got bit. Lost the middle finger on her right hand.

You know what happens when you get a snake bite? First ya' feel this burning under the skin, and then the flesh begins to swell till it's stiff and hard. Like there's something under the surface that just can't wait to get uncovered and you'd slice your very skin to let it out. At least, that's how Miah described it.

That's what this feels like. This having a calling that you can't share. This knowing who you are and pretending what you're not. It's like a bite. Only the swelling is happening in your heart.

(She shoves the ribbon into the pocket of her robe.)

I've carried a word from God in my belly till it ached with not being born . . . till it weighed on my back and pushed on my lungs . . . till it squirmed inside me in the dark of night. Whether it's poison or promise, I can't say. But it has to come out or your throat will grow so thick with words you choke. Your hands'll do things you don't even recognize. Cut your own wrists to let out the pressure . . . tear out your hair to make room. But that Word'll keep growin' and growin', till the pain collects in your ankles and throbs behind your eyes.

Sometimes, I think, God means to break our hearts . . .

(She sinks to the floor.)

. . . to give us words none'll believe or let us say. The words strain in silence, till they become the sound of a heart bust all to pieces. A teacup on concrete. It's the music of heaven, that sound, hearts breakin' with beauty 'fore the throne of God. It's a music can drive a person mad. And it hurts like hell.

And then one day, when you can't carry the weight no more, you get a sign, callin' from the Grundy's front yard. And you come home with the only pulpit you will ever call your own. A grace from God when there was nothin' left a' you to shatter.

(Rising.)

I keep it in the garage, so no one sees, and sneak down here sometimes at night. I pull off the tarp that keeps it clean and I stand behind it.

(She does this. The pulpit is a collage of glass and color . . . robin's egg blue underneath, gold leaf accents, mosaics of china, pieces of fabric and feathers. It looks like a crazy quilt. Vibrant, carefully designed, but still recognizable in shape.)

So close I can feel the Spirit breathing under the wood. I never stood on the speaking side of another.

But this one is mine. I'm the lone soul sees 'er fer what she is . . . hidden away in the dark. We know each other by name, this pulpit and me. I sanded her down and made 'er pretty. I sacrificed for her, like the woman perfuming Jesus's feet. Broke every piece of my mama's china—the ones she handed over as a consolation prize when she gave up on my ever havin' a weddin' day. Smashed 'em on this very floor 'n gave 'em new birth. Mama still asks me why I don't use em.

(She caresses the pulpit as she speaks.)

I chose a robin's egg blue to cover her scars. The color of a shell waitin' to burst open in spring. Sometimes I think she shimmers like snakeskin. Jeremiah would be proud.

(She pulls the ribbon from her pocket and lays it over the pulpit's edge so the audience can see it.)

I wait in the dark. I know itsa' comin'. I hear the Spirit moaning in that grain. I feel it enter me . . . fill me. Cool Spirit water running down my limbs . . . my arms . . . my fingers. I open my mouth and my voice falls down like rain, my insides a burst cloud. The lilt of the sound running the length of my spine. My ribs split like a pistachio shell to free my lungs.

(*As she speaks, she removes the slippers from her feet and the hairclips in her hair. She lets her bathrobe drop to the ground and stands barefoot in a simple white cotton shift.*)

I shed my skin 'n stand in the moonlight poolin' on the ground, feeling for all the world like I did on my baptism day.

I preach then. I preach to the lawnmower. To the garden tools and my old Dodge station wagon.

(*With ecstatic urgency, she turns the lawn chairs to face her pulpit and stands behind it.*)

I preach to the termites in the wall and the spider in the corner. I preach till my words lose all their sense.

(*Preaching now, with authority.*)

Children a' earth and heirs a' heaven, return to the Word you know in yer heart . . . the Word that is near. The Word that pulses in your veins and fills your stomach like bread. Who will remember and stand and speak? There is a Word that lives . . . that beats even now in yer frightened heart. Hear it. Cry it out like a dog in heat. Don't be shamed to look a fool . . . open yer mouth and be filled.

(*She collects herself, coming out from behind pulpit.*)

What does it matter that no one hears? That the trash cans and boxes of Christmas lights sit silent and deaf? What does it matter that the words fall hard on a dirty floor? Most preachers spend their lives sowing words in the soil of hearts twice as hard. Fillin' the ears of people just as deaf. The point ain't being heard. The point is speaking. Everybody needs a pulpit. It's the joy and ache 'a living.

(*She pauses.*)

I found Jeremiah in the forest at our secret meetin' place when she was twenty-eight years old—cold, stone dead.

(While she speaks, she slowly ties Jeremiah's ribbon to another piece of ribbon on her pulpit, making it part of the whole.)

Snake bite in both her hands like the nail wounds of Jesus.

(With hard-fought hope.) She was smiling.

The Word

"But Mary treasured up all these things, pondering them in her heart." Luke 2:19

(A woman sits on a stool, reading a book. The book is filled with ribbons, threads, and scraps of cloth that serve as bookmarks. She is dressed in modern clothing and wears a blue, decorative scarf, styled in a current fashion. Around her are stacks of books of every kind: art, science, philosophy, theology, and fiction—as well as a cup of tea.)

Oh, this is where it gets good.

(She reads aloud—tongue-in-cheek.)

"For it is no true wisdom that you offer your disciples, but only its semblance; for by writing to them . . . without teaching them, you make them seem to know much, while for the most part, they know nothing. And as men filled, not with wisdom, but with the conceit of wisdom, they will be *(with sarcastic emphasis)* a burden to their fellows."[1]

(Addressing the audience with a smile, she holds up the book.)

A bit overharsh, don't you think? Plato's *Phaedrus* . . . discussing the invention of writing and its danger for humankind. Such cheek. Dismissing all booklovers as a "burden." I think he protests too much for someone writing

1. R. Hackenforth, trans., *Plato's Phaedrus* (Cambridge: Cambridge University Press, 1952), 157.

a book! Which is why they made me the Divine Keeper of Manuscripts. Nobody loves this library more than me.

(She looks around with genuine delight.)

You didn't know the afterlife had a library, did you? I won't waste my time explaining the metaphysics of it all. But it's a treasury. A divine labor of love. I shouldn't give Plato such a hard time. He preferred the "living word" of a really good teacher—as do I. But I've always found the Living Word that I love to be tucked into ordinary, material things—like text on a page. These words aren't dead like Plato thinks. They work on me, making space in my heart for whispers of a Spirit bigger than the words themselves.

(She starts to organize the stacks around her—returning her book to its rightful place.)

It is one of the great joys of heaven to pursue the calling for which you were born. I never learned to read on earth. I was an undercover scholar. But the church knew it—even if they never used those words exactly. Medieval painters were constantly painting me with books. One had me reading on the back of the donkey! *(She settles again onto her stool.)* And now, here I sit, glorying in the goodness of a God who lifts up the lowly to know the joys of learning and scholarship . . . the *written* word. Plato took it for granted.

He still does. Writing makes us forgetful, he says. Sacrifices memory for ink-splotches. Well, I've been reading nearly two thousand years, and my memory is fine.

In fact, a little scrap of text can make the memory live. I remember the light from a star bright enough to make you forget it was shining on the night of a new moon. I remember the smell of animals and campfire smoke. The calluses on my husband's hand. I remember it was cold. One side of the stable—if you could call it that—was open to the sky. But I wasn't cold. I suppose it's hard to get cold in the middle of labor.

(She rouses herself from her memory and picks up her cup of tea, smiling.)

This is a second great joy of heaven. They allow tea in the library.

(Continuing) All those myths about my pregnancy—that I never had a moment's discomfort. That's not true. I had morning sickness with the best of them. That's how I knew I hadn't dreamt the whole thing up. But I did have an easy labor. A peaceful labor. I don't mean to disappoint. Nothing tops an epic labor story. I am fully aware the whole, "my-labor-was-remarkably-simple" stuff doesn't play as well. But perhaps, when you've risked a great deal to carry the Word, when you've fought to find space to bear the Word and you've endured—when the time finally comes to birth the Word . . . you find you have everything you need.

(She returns to her former train of thought, tying it to her passion for the texts around her.)

When I look at words on a page, I see the negative imprint of a starry sky. Black stars on a white midnight. That night, I looked up through a hole in that stable wall and watched the heavens dance. The whole world was vibrating. Every bit of matter throbbed with joy and pulsed with sound. The stars themselves were singing. Words on a page can do that too. They can vibrate with song and open up like space. They're made of the same stars and dust that made up the Word I held to my breast that night. Matter and flesh, nothing more or less. Paper and ink, atoms and elements. If God could find space to live in me—why not them?

You know, scientists have studied those atoms and found that they are, in fact, mostly space.

(She picks up another book and opens it, proving her point for herself. She doesn't need to read it, though. She knows this by heart.)

In the middle of all that nothing—a tiny nucleus. But the nucleus is also mostly space. There are protons and neutrons, of course. But the proton, as well . . . mostly space. Filled with a few baubles and bits, like gluons and nuons and quarks. But quarks are also mostly space. Except—I think they've discovered this by now . . . if not, count it a boon for your research—except inside the quark, at the base of it all, there is this tiny thread of vibrating energy. And of course, anything that vibrates—*(triumphant)* makes sound.[2]

So the stars *did* sing that night—as did those stable walls—my very skin—and these dead words. We sing all of us, creatures of star and stable dust, or . . . to be more clear, we *are* a song. Space and song together. How marvelous when the poet foreshadows science's discovery, and when a woman like me, who spent so many years spinning thread from a drop spindle, finds that God is a spinner of threads, as well.

(She looks down at the book she has been holding.)

I like to imagine all those threads vibrating together—in you and me—tying our stories into a harmony just out of range of the human ear. Not every thread vibrates with joy, I know.

(She holds up a thread serving as a bookmark in her book. It is the scarlet piece of yarn cut by the blocked academic in "The Annunciation.")

2. I first heard this lovely lesson in particle physics in a sermon entitled, "Creation's Song" by Rev. Christen Harley Matlick, Miller Chapel, 1998. Her description was based on Leonard Sweet's forum on youth ministry lecture, "Living an Ancient Future Faith," Princeton Theological Seminary, April 30, 1997.

Not every thread finds a way to amplify its song into the world . . .

(She holds up a blue ribbon also serving as a bookmark. It is the blue ribbon that belonged to Jeremiah in "The Call.")

. . . at least not in a way in which anyone will ever be aware. But the threads sing all the same.

The threads of a life are precious, and so I save them.

(She closes her book with deliberate care.)

Books need bookmarks, after all. I may be the Mother of the Word . . . but I am also a mother of flesh and a loyal friend to those who, like me, bear the Word. So, I pay attention. I collect yarn and ribbons, cloth and cuttings—the threads of human testimony, and I press them between the pages of these books of mine. Between these vibrating black stars of text.

(She reveals a bundle of threads, rolled in fabric, lying on the table among the books. She lifts them to view and places them as bookmarks in the books before her.)

I see them. I catalog them. I run them through my fingers like I was spinning them myself. And I whisper over them, "You are not dead . . . just as these written words are not dead. You sing, and I hear the song."

The world is merciless with matter and flesh. If any would know this, I would know. It pretends to honor it and primp it and coddle it and worship it—but finally, it disdains it. It scorns ordinary things and ordinary people and ordinary words and, all too often . . . extraordinary Ones. It cuts down threads with all the efficiency of a scythe and clears it away like clutter—making space for the new, the more, the wondrous, the next. It takes a thread and mocks the song it sings. It stretches it upon a cross of fear and calculation. Or worse, it shrugs and turns away. It pronounces our words dead . . . our song dead.

But by the grace of God, there is another thread—a thread that stretches from the highest heaven to the lowest cattle trough. To that very cross itself. And this thread, too, vibrates. Sounding forth a note of love from God's own heart. And that pure note—with purer tone than all our tired cacophony—is the Word made flesh. The Word that is the Christ. And he will not be silenced.

He makes all sing again.

I see your faces . . . your beautiful, ordinary faces. And I know you are my daughters. You lovers of books. You keepers of threads. You bearers of the Word. I tell you a secret. The "space for God" for which you search is inside you. You were made with galaxies of space in every cell— because the Living Word wanted to fill you. And God knew the Word would need some room.

The song you want to sing, the calling of your heart, the song that takes more power than you have, more skill than you possess. The song the world has overlooked or buried under mounds of hurt, silenced by a cruel cross or simply drowned in noise . . . the song you think you lost . . . that song is humming even now under your skin, in every thread of every cell. And the question comes—to all the words and scraps and flesh of all the world: will you let the Word that is Christ tune your song? Will you let your song be the Word's song?

If you dare, it will not matter where the Word is born: a cattle trough, a book, a conversation over tea, a spiral journal filled with chicken scratch, a canvas that is never seen and canvases that are. No matter. The Word will come, and it will be enough. Enough to wake again your wonder for the world—this ordinary, broken, lovely, vibrating world. And you will find, when you have risked it all to carry that Word, when you have struggled to find space to bear that Word into the world and have endured, when time then comes to birth the Word—you will have everything you need. Space and song and God who hears. God who speaks through you.

(She closes the book on her lap.)

This is when I close my books. Such promise is too great for human words to bear. They strain under the weight of glory. Plato may have missed the wonder of the written word, but he was right about at least one thing. Some moments, only face-to-face encounters will suffice. Carrying the Word in your belly and holding the baby in your arms are very different things—related, but as different as work from worship. No human word has yet been penned that does not pale in beauty to the sound that rises when the threads of our lives sing like strings of praise around the throne of God. No angel harp compares. It is our call—and joy.

(In benediction.) Selah.

Promised Land

Author's Note:

We are used to descriptions of Mary as the perfect mother and perfect believer—but the gospels tell a more complicated story. This is a woman who struggled to understand the Word she had birthed—a woman who stood at a distance from that Word, and even lost that Word on a Passover pilgrimage. Long before she watched her son die on a cross, she heard him disown her before his followers. "Who," Jesus asked, "are my mother and brothers?" as she stood bewildered outside. And yet, in her final biblical appearance, she is surrounded by his disciples, sharing their Pentecost prayer. She is "overshadowed" by the Spirit once again. These monologues emerge from the fault lines of this experience. Is a family made up of flesh or faith? And can one honor the one without giving up on the other?

Promised Land does not attempt to retell Mary's story in modern dress. Instead, it draws out the implications of her story for our modern struggle around the boundaries, betrayals, and miracle of family. Family—at once idolized, debated, and undermined by contemporary culture—crystallizes the tension at the root of identity. Are we—and the families we claim—determined by our genetic ties or by our own powers of choice? A similar tension can be found at the root of love. In a world increasingly marked by individualism, consumerism, and tribalism, how does love call us to honor the bodily connections that tie us to community? And how does love require our transcending those bodily ties for the sake of a promise not yet seen?

A Note on Staging:

The following monologues can be preformed as stand-alone pieces or as a whole. While there are several key props needed for each scene, the pieces lend themselves to a minimalist style. For those performing the entire collection, the hive boxes in "Honey" might be used in a variety of ways in the rest of the production—as the base for the window frame in "Jordan," for example, or as a simple table that sits beside the rocking chair in "Milk." Such visual resonances between the pieces underscore the thematic unity that runs throughout. If desired, the sheets that obscure the stage at the start can also serve as screens for projected images.

Between the monologues, the sheets will be pushed aside, one by one, to reveal the setting of the next scene, with the stage becoming increasingly exposed. By the time the sheet that hides the props for "Table" is removed, the stage should have a bare quality, the remnants from the preceding scenes in view, though unlit.

(Lights come up on a stage that has been strung with clothes-lines, each at a different angle and stage depth. White sheets conceal the simple props needed for the monologues to follow. The sheet downstage-center is backlit to reveal the form of a woman. She speaks.)

When light hits a body, it leaves a shadow. No permanent record. No proof of purchase. Nothing you can hold in your hand. But the shadow is there because the body is there. The body and the light.

Families have shadows. I don't have to tell you that. You know.

If they didn't, they would be nothing but air—*(with a laugh)* which maybe you'd prefer.

But this is not a play about air. It's a play about shadows—for better or worse. About what bodies can do and what they can't—and the light that sometimes shines through.

(Tenderly, after a pause.) Breathe, now. Don't be afraid. We are safe here. There are no perfect mothers—or perfect children. But there is grace—that comes like Shadow, clinging to our bodies and to light.

(The woman pushes the curtain aside to reveal the hives in "Honey." She dons a beekeeper's hat that is lying on top of a hive, and picks up a bee smoker.)

Honey

"Someone told Jesus, 'Look, your mother and brothers
are standing outside, wanting to speak with you.' But
. . . he replied, 'Who are my mother and brothers?'"
Matthew 12:48

(Woman is standing behind a stack of honey hives. Several
lay beside her with their tops removed. She is dressed in a
beekeeper's protective clothing—including a netted hat that
covers her face. The net obstructs, but does not conceal her
expression. She holds a smoker and smokes the hive as she
talks to the bees.)

Calm down. I haven't done this in awhile. I forget how
much of this stuff you need. Doesn't seem like it should
work. You'd think smoke would make a beehive nervous,
not keep you quiet.

Some crazy déjà vu. It could be twenty years ago. Me
out here on a Saturday morning wondering why we can't
just buy the plastic honey-bear squirt bottle from Hy-Vee.
Dad would never have stood for that. You were his favorites.
You could get away with anything—even a slow production
year. No ketchup in *our* house—which is near sacrilege in
this part of the country. He put honey on his potatoes—
hurt my teeth just to watch.

I don't think he even wanted a family—just a hive.
Everybody following orders—playing a role. He used to tell

his church that family was about faith, not blood. You just believe your way in. Which sounds nice until you believe your way out. He was watching TV when I left for the last time—never even looked up.

(*She closes the top of the hive and sits on an empty crate beside them.*)

It wasn't the last time, was it? You'd think one of the trade-offs of being a disowned daughter is not having to do the death march at the end.

If it weren't for you, I wouldn't have come back. I find a dead bee in my wine glass one night, and the call from hospice comes the next morning. Like it was an omen or something.

I couldn't sleep. I'd dream I was walking through some smoky house and find you swarming in the cupboards. My girlfriend found me crying at some CNN story on this "Colony Collapse" business. Whole hives of honeybees getting confused and forgetting their way home. Even you all are getting dementia.

(*With a deep breath, she continues. Very matter of fact. She pulls up the netting on her face.*)

When a beekeeper dies—somebody tells the bees. That's the rule, right? Every almanac says so. Every beekeeping trivia collection. Mama's gone. He's driven off anybody that loved him. This shouldn't be my job. You're the ones who hitched your wagon to a failed preacher nobody could stand.

But here I am, after all these years. Coming halfway across the country to break it to the queen.

(*A pause.*)

Maybe I owe it to you.

(*She becomes very still.*)

He's not coming back. That's what I'm here to say. He's laying up in the house, bones and skin, like twigs under a sheet. He's still breathing, but he doesn't remember you—or me. So, find yourself a new keeper. I'd like to tell you he's replaceable. That you choose who you belong to. *(Shrugging.)* That's what he told *me*.

But dads are hard to come by—even when you're born to them. You get what you get—and you have very little say in the matter. Even now—when he has nothing to say about anything anymore.

(She stands, addressing the hives with frustration.)

The hospice woman asked me today if I wanted to cut his hair. I just stared at her. She held out the scissors so hopefully, as if this is what good daughters do. They come home and stroke dad's head and run their fingers through whatever is left and make him presentable. We never touched when I lived under his roof. And I haven't touched him since. To touch now seems a lie about who we were . . . and are. I didn't come home to pretend.

(She grows quiet.)

That's not true, you know . . . that he never touched me. There was one time I was six and got a bee sting. I'd been watching him fill your feeders with antibiotic.

(She crosses to a glass bee feeder hanging on its stand near the hive, fingering it as she continues. She acts out the scene.)

I felt something light on my hair, and I flicked at it and got stung. It was my first time, and I howled like dog. He took my hand. He had these rough leather gloves, but I could imagine his skin underneath. He lifted my finger to his lips—and sucked. Hard. He pinched the spot till a little bead of blood showed and sucked again. Stunned me silent. I hardly ever felt his touch on my skin—never his lips. His honey was the only sweetness in him. But that day he held my hand and sucked the stinger out of my finger like he gave a damn.

(Her anger flares.)

Your hives are the only things on this place with a clean coat of paint. The only things not falling apart. Nothing's changed. Why do you think I put dish soap in these jars *(taking down the bee feeder)* all those years ago? Why do you think I wanted you dead? Blood relations matter to most folks. Family matters. What kind of daughter loses out to a hive?

Don't worry. I learned my lesson. His face shut like a trap. The next day I found honey smeared all over my rabbits—every one of them crawling with bees. Not one made it.

(A quiet tension builds amid the gentle buzzing.)

This is why I didn't want to come back. I knew you'd plead for mercy.

(She sets the bee feeder down deliberately, as if it might break. She is tired of the anger.)

He never mentioned it—so I didn't either. Not even the day I left. I think he regretted it. Being absent and angry is different from being cruel. *(Pause.)* Just not as different as you'd think.

(She makes a decision within herself, crosses to the hive and carefully slides aside the top. She stands back a few feet as she speaks.)

I liked his face when he was around you. I should thank you for that. I liked working here beside him. I liked the feel of scooping you into a cardboard box when you'd swarm and we'd find you balled up in the orchard.

(She closes her eyes as she remembers.)

Lifting the mound of you like we were cradling kittens. I'd let your weight rest in my hands. Holding you without holding you. Scared of your sting—but awed by your trust. The way you hung on, confused, when you'd spent your lives avoiding my fingers.

(She opens her eyes and reaches out a hand to touch the edge of the hive—capturing some sticky-sweet residue on her glove. She reveals a secret that is hard to say.)

Today, he was breathing hard. He smelled sour and there was spit on his cheek. I put my arm under the crook of his neck, and I held him as if he were you.

(She crosses slowly downstage, and as she speaks, she removes her glove—getting some of the honey on her fingers in the process.)

Holding him without holding him. Letting his weight rest in my hands.

Blood matters in the end. Blood and body, when all else fails.

He looked at me like he knew me—though I knew he couldn't have. *(Simply.)* And he didn't look away.

(She lifts a hand to her mouth to suck a drop of honey from a fingertip—as if she is sucking out a stinger.)

Jordan

"And Jesus said . . . 'Did you not know I must be in my Father's house?'" Luke 2:49

(A window frame with open shutters is built above a window seat. The whole unit is turned backward so that the seat faces upstage and the shutters face the audience. Behind the window are the essentials of a young girl's bedroom—a small table and bed.

A woman bursts into the room. She is wearing work clothes, tight and a little dated, with large sunglasses and a bag slung over her shoulder. She is boiling mad. She searches for her daughter throughout the room—throwing back bed covers and looking under the bed. She is doing more yelling than searching. Her daughter could be anywhere in the house.)

Jordan? Jordan! Where are you? I have to go. I have to drop you at Mee-Maw's in ten minutes or I'm gonna be late. Come out now or you're gonna get it! *(Taking on a cloying tone)* You want Skittles? I got Skittles *(searching frantically through her bag, under her breath)* . . . in here somewhere.

(Out of the bag and onto the table come candies of all sorts . . . Pixy Stix, Laffy Taffy, Tootsie Rolls . . . also cigarettes. She tries to induce guilt.)

Baby, you're making Mama smoke . . . Mama's getting cancer. *(She lights up.)* JORDAN! Baby Dylan's ready to go.

He's going to start squawking any minute. I swear to God if he starts screaming—you're screaming too. Come out NOW.

(Nothing. She alternates emotional tacks at whiplash pace.)

Honey, we'll get a Big Gulp on the way home. Don't make me yell. You want a chili dog from Jack's? Let's get out of here. You're gonna to make Mama lose her job.

(Silence. She slouches onto the bed—frustrated. She thinks she is alone.)

Jordan Keeling, you are a worthless waste of space. *(She notices a movement outside the window and, after a moment of recognition, she scrambles up surprised.)* Whoa. Oh my God. Don't go any further. Jordan. Stop climbing. *(Frantic.)* How did you get out there?

(She moves to the window seat and sticks her head out of the frame, looking up and down. Her daughter has been listening to her tirade from a tree outside—two stories up. The girl has moved higher and is out reach—pretending to read, so as to ignore her mother. From this point on, when the woman speaks to her daughter, she kneels on the seat and leans through the open window—her face slightly raised. She is apologetic.)

Baby, Mama didn't mean it. You know I didn't. Now come on down, let's go.

(She considers climbing out of the window herself, reaches for a branch but decides it impossible. Her tone turns conspiratorial. She is wary of neighbors.)

Jordan, you know I can't come out there after you. There's no way that tree limb is holding me. *(Looking down)* That's a two-story drop. I don't even know how you did it. You're crazy. Jordan, pay attention to me. You can stare at that book all you want. I know you're not reading up there. You're not fooling anybody. You are going to fall—and I'm the one who's gonna get in trouble. What do you want—to give your dad more ammunition? The judge already likes him better—'cause, you know, unemployed screwups make the best fathers. Jordan, get your nose out of the book and look at me. It's you and me against the world. *(Pausing, determined.)* I'm not going to lose you because you're feeling sorry for yourself and went tree climbing.

(She leans far out the window, trying to demand attention.)

Look at me. I know you can hear me. I do not like you ignoring me. Stop staring at that book and climb down. You can give me the silent treatment in the car.

(She breathes deep and decides to try a more calm approach.)

You are only going Mee-Maw's for a few days. Just so I can work overnight. I'll catch up on my sleep and come pick you up. Not like last time. I won't even stop at Jesse's on the way home—though I could use the down time. Wednesday afternoon, cross my heart. *(Pleading now.)* Jordan, Mee-Maw's not so bad. You can't take what she says personally. Just shrug her off. Or yell back. You gotta suck it up. She's family, OK.

She behaved herself yesterday—except for that business with your flip-flops. Who had your back, Jordan? How else was the church gonna see your purple toenails? Right? She's lucky you were getting baptized at all. She got what she wanted. Doesn't matter one bit what kind of shoes you were wearing.

(With refocused energy) Jordan, I can make you come down from there. I can go borrow a ladder. *(A tense pause, then a desperate whisper.)* Jordan, don't make me borrow a ladder. That government lady has been poking around. The hearing is next week. You *want* people to say I'm a bad mom? You want them to take you away, so you can live

with Mee-Maw for good? Mamas yell sometimes. They lose their tempers. I lose my temper. I make mistakes, OK. Get over it. I live here on this planet—not whatever Jesus-happy world you're from.

(She squints and recognizes the book Jordan is reading.)

Oh God. That's what you're reading, isn't it? The Bible they gave you. Jordan, you are up a tree with a Bible. That's just Stephen King weird. Do not do this to me. *(With escalating anger.)* You and this Jesus thing has to stop. I am your mother. You belong to me. I don't care that some preacher lady put water on your head and said some magic words. I'm not having you brainwashed. Church is not what it's cracked up to be. How do you think Mee-Maw got so mean? You think those people loving on you yesterday are gonna be around when you need them? That preacher acting like she was your mama or something—she doesn't know you like I do. I'm what you got. I'm the one working the extra shift. I'm the one who left your dad when he was drinking bad . . . *(grimly)* I'm the one hanging out a window two stories up, talking to tree.

(Considering, she puts out her cigarette on the sill and swings her legs awkwardly over the side. She sits on the edge of the sill, her legs dangling—holding tight to the frame.)

I get it, OK? I get it's important to you. I get you want to be princess for a day. But you're not grown—and you're not a baby anymore either. A bit of water doesn't change anything.

(She still receives no response.)

You're not the only one that's important. You never even looked at me yesterday. Just stood there in your own little world. *(Her volume grows.)* You embarrassed? You want to leave me too? You won't even look at me *now*! You won't even pretend I matter.

Just like your father. Don't kid yourself.

(She struggles to climb back inside.)

You hear me, Jordan. You hear me good. Water and words don't make you family. Pretending don't make you family.

(She faces her daughter. Her voice is taut.)

What makes you family is when some social worker is sitting in your hospital room, handing you papers between contractions to sign over your baby. And you're alone and your mama's not going to lift one finger to help. And you're sure it's right. And the nurse asks if you want to see her before they take her away. What makes you family is that she puts you in my arms and I look in your eyes and know *(fiercely)* . . . you belong . . . to *me*. You can't take that away from me, Jordan. Not even God himself can take that away from me. I would like to see him try.

(Deliberately, she locks the shutters—and leaves the room.)

Milk

"Woman, here is your son." John 19:26

(Woman sits in a rocking chair. She has a baby in her arms, wrapped in a blanket. The baby is asleep. She speaks to the audience in the plain, expository style of testimony.)

She was my soldier girl. Short, black hair and perfect aim. We met in boot camp. Took my heart without even asking. I can still hear her breathing in the bunk above. My heart beats fast just thinking about it. Sneaking around, kissing in the stalls.

Then she got pregnant. A one-night thing, she said. Some dive bar, some greasy surfer-guy. But she wanted the baby. She wanted everything the world could give her.

I broke it off. Too complicated. I wanted a career fixing V-22 Osprey helicopters. She wanted to fight.

I didn't expect her to show up on my doorstep, baby in hand. Her orders had come up, and she was headed out. "I can't leave him with my mom," she said. And that part was true. Kris's mom smelled of cigarettes, and her eyes were mean.

"Mamas don't do this," I said. "You take maternity leave and wait. You mother your baby." But she didn't listen. "It's just six months," she said. "The war might be over next year. They got daycare on base—you can do this." And I knew I could. I knew I would. And she knew it too. She didn't have to say, "Do it for us." The words were an unspoken promise between us. You believe in stuff like that when she's your first.

So, she dropped off the car seat and a used Pack-and-Play. Made sure I knew how to use the diapers. Conner was still in the three-month size when I got him. Small for his age. He'd been breast-feeding, but Kris said he liked formula too. How hard could it be, right? I could fix the most complicated aviation engine in the Marine Corps. I could do this.

But it's harder than it looks. Everybody says that, but it's true. Especially alone. The first three nights he did nothing but cry. He kept fighting the bottle. His whole face would scrunch up, like the nipple was sour. I bought some different ones at the grocery store. Conner screaming as I walked up and down the baby aisle. Mothers looking at me with sympathetic eyes, but I couldn't tell them what I'd done. Signed on for a six-month babysitting gig for a woman who had already broken my heart.

Conner didn't want any of them—the new nipples I mean. That first week, I took sick leave from work and let him suck the formula off my fingers. I was ready to take him to the doctor when I decided to put my own nipple in his mouth. I had nothing to give, of course, but he started sucking for all he was worth. He was quiet for the first time in three days. Maybe he needed the touch more than anything. Maybe he was like his mom—who liked the struggle more than the win. We were both asleep in ten minutes flat, joined at the breast.

It got easier after that. Conner started eating from his bottle during the day. And I'd drop him off at daycare each morning. But at night, all he wanted was me. He craved my body like air—like a drug. He wouldn't sleep without it. I felt strange at first. Like maybe I was out-of-bounds. I wasn't his mom. He wasn't mine. I hadn't carried him. Maybe I didn't have the right. Kris would write these quick notes from Afghanistan, and I would have twinges of guilt—but mostly, they passed. She wrote once that her breasts had been leaking milk so bad, she had to empty them into the ground on break—just to get rid of the pain. The Afghan women whispered about it, she said. Some of them laughed.

Such a waste. Milk in the dirt. And here I sat in a dark room, holding her baby to an empty breast—both of us wanting something we couldn't have.

(Pause.)

There's a butterfly migration that happens every year in San Diego. Thousands of them cross the border. For a few weeks, you stand still and count a dozen fly by. It was the day after Easter I got the news. I wasn't family—so I hadn't been told right away. It was the lawyer who called me. Female Engagement Teams aren't usually in the line of fire. But there had been a roadside bomb. The whole truck had flipped. Kris had named me Conner's guardian. She'd failed to mention it—which was crazy—and just like her. I'm sure she never thought there'd be a need.

I stood on the front lawn. Butterflies loping through the air like hurt birds fighting for lift. Headed away.

Bodies can't be something they're not. Babysitting's a far cry from family. Kris wasn't coming back. And I had a baby in my house that I'd known for eight weeks.

I never cried when she cheated on me. I never cried when Conner kept me up three nights straight, and I was ready to throw my coffee at the wall. I never cried when the lawyer called. News of good soldiers dying went through the camp every week. But that night, when Conner clamped onto my chest, I cried.

It hurts at first. Baby has to toughen your nipple, they say. But those late nights after I got the news, it was a good kind of hurt. Like he was sucking the poison out of me. Sucking out tears that wouldn't come any other way. He'd turn me inside out, and I could feel again. No pretending about Kris and me. No pretending to be something I wasn't. No pretending at all. Just our bodies connected. Him watching my face with his brown eyes.

I don't believe in miracles. I've spent every year since I was sixteen building engines. Bolts matter. Wiring matters. Bodies matter. Machines can't do what they haven't been built to do. People, the same way.

But sometimes things that aren't supposed to happen, do.

You're listening to the hum of metal, and you hear something more than gears and belts. You hear the motor breathing—whispering something you can't quite hear.

Conner'll be watching me and I get this dizzy feeling in the back of my brain—like warm water trickling down the back of my neck—like the fizz of a Coke only warmer and soft. My head won't stand up straight, and my eyes get slow and still. Like I'm floating under water—but with clothes on—everything heavy and sweet. My chest prickling with pins. And then, it comes.

Don't ask me how it happens. I hear some moms work to nurse their babies for months and never let down. I don't have any business making milk. It's a malfunction. (*A quiet laugh.*) The first time he latched off all surprised, and I kept squirting into his face like a leaky hose. He knows better now. His eyes get wide for second, and he breathes sharp through his nose like he's startled. But he doesn't let go. (*With a smile.*) He gets down to business.

So I don't know.

(*She looks at Conner now, holding him so she can see his face.*)

I don't know anymore what makes a family—whether its blood or milk. Or a miracle.

Maybe a family is whoever you feed.

(She unbuttons her shirt and puts the child to her breast—helping him latch on.)

Table

"All with one mind were devoting themselves to prayer,
along with the women, and Mary the mother of Jesus.
. . . When the day of Pentecost came, they were all
together in one place." Acts 1:14, 2:1

(A woman in her sixties is surrounded by charred wood. She
is dressed in a clergy collar, standing in the burned out hull
of a church. Sun pours through a hole in the roof. Behind her
leans the burnt remains of a communion table. She speaks to
the audience as to a confessor.)

When light hits a body, it leaves a shadow. No permanent record. No proof of purchase. Nothing you can hold
in your hand.

(Pause.)

I didn't expect glory.

Preachers are trained to look for small signs of life that
no one sees, the weeds in the cracks, and call it resurrection
(smiling ruefully) instead of erosion.

But there comes a day that doesn't cut it anymore.

You lose confidence in holy things when you handle
them for a living. You see the Welch's grape juice contain-
er—the day-old communion bread bought on special.

In the beginning, you pay attention to their hands.
When they come forward, you notice the fingers that trem-
ble—or a child's palm.

But over time, they all look the same. Ungrateful, grasping. Unworthy of even the bargain bread. Your compassion wears thin for this dysfunctional clan—and you think, this isn't what I signed on for—to babysit the tired and afraid.

(She sits on a broken piece of the communion rail.)

No one tells you what it's going to cost. You think you know when you start. You think you know what the hardest part will be. The always being on call. The ugly wallpaper in the parsonage kitchen. The Finance Committee Chair. You think you know.

But the hardest part is the love. It would be easier without that. You could harden your heart or walk away. You could say you don't care about them anymore. But you do.

I would look at them—their dwindling numbers—their disappointed stares, and I so wanted to tell them—let's tear this place down. Let's get out of here. All of us together. You would look different in the sunlight. Your faces would look different. Maybe you wouldn't look so sad. So angry at this sanctuary that used to be full, falling down around your ears.

(With irony, she shakes her head at what she has just said. She is still in shock.)

I used to fantasize about burning this place to the ground. But in the fantasy, there was nothing to lose.

(Pause.)

I got the call at four in the morning. The insurance folks blame faulty wiring—which sounds entirely likely. The place is over a hundred years old. By the time I got here, you could see the flames four blocks away.

(She crouches down and picks up a pile of ash at her feet.)

Table   53

The carved communion chalice Earle made in his woodshop. The felt Sunday School banners. *(With irony.)* The comprehensive minutes of the Women's Society.

The table.

(She stands and places the handful of ash on the table's charred surface.)

Handmade in the late 1800s, I'm told—by an old, bachelor member. Carved cherry wood. Unlike any table I'd seen. It had these handcrafted vines curled around the sides, and if you looked close, an occasional carved insect—like a moth. Or some sort of friendly beetle.

When I watched it burn, I kept seeing the table in my mind. A labor of love shooting up flame. A hundred years ago, they called them "altars." My stripe of Protestant doesn't do that anymore. It's a "table." But who are we fooling? Table or altar—it all ends up ash.

We have no idea what we're playing at in these bodies of ours. We promise things we can't give and break each other's hearts. Then fire comes, and I'm standing beside of a seventy-eight-year-old organist in a parking lot, listening to her organ pipes groan as they burn.

(She gives a resigned shrug, remembering her prior reflection.)

The hardest part is the love.

(Touching the table.) It seems to fit us now—with all its scars. It doesn't pretend. Like that preacher who stood in the pulpit, dying of some dread disease, and preached his final sermon. I spent my ministry wishing I could be that honest. Maybe now.

(Pause.)

I felt a Shadow on my face the day I was called. I knew God saw me—and the Word was near.

But the betrayals come, and the compromises. The Word seems silent—and all you have left are their imperfect hands. Their heavy bodies blocking out the light. I chose faith. Every year, I made some new Good Friday pledge—but I wished I could feel that Shadow one more time.

(She catches a glimpse of her own shadow on the floor.)

Suddenly, I see them everywhere—shadows. It's the hole in the roof—the sun reflecting off smoke. But I'm startled by their coolness—the way they cling to my hands.

(She is moving her hands in the air now—slowly, transfixed. She stills herself.)

Maybe It was here all along.

(She moves behind the table—as if she is going to offer up the Great Thanksgiving. But she speaks simply, as one who has nothing to prove—only speaking what she knows.)

In the oldest Christian liturgies, the table didn't only hold bread and wine—it held milk and honey too. The food of promised land, drawing the congregation toward the future, like moths to a burning wick.

(She speaks the only promise she has left to give.)

The future is a table, where fathers and daughters, lovers and friends—and even enemies—sit. Their faces glowing. The shadows of their imperfect hands, dancing like flame.

(The lighting shifts, illuminating the entire stage, with the shadow of the woman, arms outstretched, coming into focus on the back wall.)

Breathe now. Don't be afraid. There are no perfect families. But there is grace that comes like Shadow, clinging to our bodies and to light.

(Fade to black.)

Reflection Questions for *Space for God* and *Promised Land*

Some of the most powerful moments in theater come, not on stage, but in the discussion of the audience following the piece. Preachers have long been familiar with a congregation's uncanny ability to hear resonances in sermons that were unintended. These resonances are part of the Word's proclamation.

The preceding pieces have been performed in theaters, seminary forums, women's retreats, and Christian education settings. Several have played a part in worship services. I have been humbled by the quality of the discussions that regularly follow and have concluded that these discussions are part of the pieces themselves. The questions I offer here grow out of the Christian biblical witness and most are devotional in nature. They are not the right questions for every crowd. But I hope they serve as a springboard for those ready to reflect on the greater Shadow at work within the ordinary shadows of life. The goal is not to articulate some singular "meaning" in the work. The goal is to prayerfully listen for the voice of that greater Shadow, speaking through and to the gathered community.

Space for God:

"The Annunciation," in response to Luke 1:26–38

1. In your own life, which has been more common: moments when you were called to speak a Word difficult for others to hear—or moments when you feared you didn't have any Word worth speaking at all? Which experience was harder for you?

2. What is currently taking up the "space for God" in your life?

3. What new thing might God want to birth in you?

4. What would you need to lay down in order for God to do this work?

"The Call," in response to Luke 2:1–7, Jeremiah 20:7–9

1. What do you think of this woman's decision to preach in a garage? Is it a sign of courage or cowardice?

2. At one point she says, "I think sometimes God means to break our hearts." Do you believe this is true? Why would God give a Word to a woman when God knows the Word will be difficult to birth?

3. The speaker says, "The point ain't bein' heard. The point is speakin'." How do you react to this statement?

4. What are the ways our academic/cultural/religious communities resist the birth of the Word in the world?

5. How can we create birthing space for those laboring around us?

6. Has your calling been a source of self-fulfillment or has it cost your life? Is there a connection between the two?

"The Word," in response to Luke 2:16–20

1. What is your current attitude toward the written word? Do you experience it as dead or alive?

2. Share a moment in your life when, unexpectedly, you had all you needed to bear a Word you did not think possible.

3. What threads in your life do you fear have been lost or wasted? What difference might it make to believe that these threads of testimony are precious to God?

4. How is the work of your life related to your worship? How is it distinct?

Promised Land:

"Honey," in response to Matthew 12:46–50

1. How do you imagine Mary felt upon hearing Jesus's question to his followers, "Who are my mother and brothers?"

2. Jesus claims that anyone who "does the will of the Father" is his family. Do you feel embraced by this statement—or worried by it? If this is the definition of spiritual family, can one be disowned?

3. Why do you think the woman returns to "tell the bees"?

4. The woman states, "Blood matters in the end." Do you agree? Is a family something we make or something that we are born into?

"Jordan," in response to Luke 2:41–52

1. After losing track of her son on a Passover pilgrimage, being sick with worry, and finding him unperturbed about the situation, Mary "could not understand" (v. 50) Jesus' response that he was "in his Father's house" (v. 49). What do you think would have been the hardest part of this situation to "understand"?

2. The mother in this piece tells her daughter, "You belong *to me*." How do you see this attitude played out in our culture's relationship to children?

3. Why is the church so threatening to the mother?

4. Does baptism change people? Families? How would you hope baptism changes Jordan and her situation?

"Milk," in response to John 19:25–27

1. In what ways do "body and blood" matter in this story—and in what ways are they unimportant?

2. Do you think that Jesus's giving of Mary and John to each other was comforting for them—or difficult? What do you imagine to be the challenges and joys of living into this new reality?

3. Share a time in your life when you were "adopted" by a group or family to which you previously didn't belong.

"Table," in response to Acts 1:13–14; 2:1–3

1. What are holy things you take for granted because you handle them everyday?

2. In the Pentecost account, "tongues of fire" represent the presence of the Spirit. How is the church-fire in this piece related to Pentecost fire? How is it distinct?

3. What wisdom do you imagine Mary brings to the disciples on the day of Pentecost? Are there things she knows, because of her experience with the Spirit and the Word, that they are just beginning to learn? What wisdom might the disciples have to offer her?

4. How do you think the fire will alter the way this clergy-woman pastors her congregation? What has changed for her and her community?

5. The Scriptures describe the Spirit as both fire and shadow. Which image resonates more with you? Are they related? Is there a time in your life when you felt the Spirit's "overshadowing" presence?

6. What is your hope for imperfect families, churches, and communities? Is this hope only a promise for the future—or does it touch down in the present? What does grace look like in this world?

Appendix: Theater as Sermon

Challenges and Possibilities:

I am, first and foremost, a preacher—not a playwright. And so, not long into this process of creative writing, the question came: are these monologues sermons? Is my performance of them "preaching"? Each of the monologues in this collection grew out of engagement with Scripture— sometimes argumentative engagement—but always prayerful engagement. And each of the texts was written to make space for questions of faith and voices of testimony. But in truth (with the exception of "The Word"), I did not write these pieces to be sermons. I wrote them as theater, and despite extended reflection on the overlap between theater and proclamation in homiletics, I have found a life-giving tension in their distinction.

Years ago, I made the decision to preach a sermon on the Twenty-Third Psalm by writing a story about a pastor who was performing a funeral service for a longtime member. This short-story sermon was an account of this clergywoman's questions and hopes for the family to whom she was ministering—and in good literary form, Psalm 23 provided the thematic structure for the plot, as well as the scriptural text for this fictitious pastor's funeral sermon. It was a carefully crafted narrative, reflecting the text like a mirror within a mirror—and I thought, at the time, it provided way for my congregation to experience this familiar passage with fresh ears. Several days later, however, I spoke to one of my most attentive listeners in the congregation and asked for feedback. "I missed you speaking directly to us," she said. "It wasn't as bold as your other sermons. It was well written, but you felt far away." She was right.

There is a longing in the church for preachers who are brave and vulnerable enough, in the words of Anna Carter Florence, to testify to what they see in the text and what they believe about it. The goal is not to "'show or tell' our side of the story," she states, "but to be formed by the Other"—to be converted.[1] Such speech requires direct address from an authentic presence within the role of preacher. It requires the possibility that the preacher be changed by the Word she speaks. I do think such speech is possible in theatrical performance. But it is very difficult. When I work with preaching students, I find it challenging enough to help them speak authentically in the role of pastor. To speak authentically from within a dramatic character, while still speaking from one's particularity in service to the gathered congregation, is often a bridge too far.

Even more challenging is writing theatrical pieces that are pastorally faithful to the scriptural text and the congregational context. Many have pointed out the tendency of first-person sermons to construct the psyche of a biblical character out of the psyche of the preacher. But the opposite danger—the eclipse of the preacher and the congregation—is also real. Richard Lischer rightfully points out that "what gives the biblical story its edge is its capacity for being told by someone embedded in a different time and place."[2] Many

1. Anna Carter Florence, *Preaching as Testimony* (Louisville: Westminster John Knox, 2007) 92.

2. Richard Lischer, *The End of Words: The Language of Reconciliation in a Culture of Violence* (Grand Rapids: Eerdmans, 2005) 114.

first-person sermons work from the assumption that their goal is to reconstruct the past, rather than speak a living promise that touches down in the present.

I recount these dangers as evidence of how difficult it is to blend these two forms. Many attempts, including my own, have resulted in poor theater and poor proclamation. But I would argue, despite the challenges, rich theological discoveries are made at the boundary between theater and preaching. This boundary is fluid—even as it is stubbornly real. Standing at the border, I find there are things I can say in one medium for which I cannot find words in the other. New understandings of performance emerge, enhancing the way I view both.[3]

Dramatic representation can introduce diverse voices that would otherwise be absent from a congregational context. It can challenge a congregation more concretely than would be possible through direct address. The open-ended quality of theater can encourage congregational conversation in ways that enhance understanding. It can provide space to discuss a controversial subject and find common ground. Each of these possibilities illuminates significant areas of conversation in the homiletic field—and each comes into focus because a preacher risks asking hard questions about the boundaries and shape of the proclaimed Word.

And so, with some trepidation, on behalf of brave souls exploring this boundary between dramatic and sermonic speech, I offer several preliminary suggestions.

- *You are preaching a sermon. Prepare as such.* Exegetical work (i.e., critically engaging both text and congregation) is a necessary part of dramatic monologue

3. Jana Childers makes her case that "a little confusion" between theater and preaching "might . . . be good for the soul" in *Performing the Word: Preaching as Theatre* (Nashville: Abingdon, 1998) 36.

sermons. Don't sell this step short. You still need a controlling idea. You still need to do justice to what the text says in light of the congregation's need and not simply recreate your response to it. By this standard, not every monologue in this collection works as a sermon in the broad context of a Sunday morning service. That does not make them wrong—or prohibit the Spirit's work through them. It simply means they were not written to address the crucible of a particular congregation's life. On the other hand, in a different context, the same monologues can speak a distinct sermonic promise. Attentiveness and prayer are essential to this discernment process.

- *Allow for the bending of time and space in your performance.* Consider transposing the biblical text into a modern key or have a biblical character speak directly to the congregation—offering exhortation as part of the "cloud of witnesses." A sermon does not simply recreate the story the congregation has just heard in the text. A sermon presses that story against the wounds and hopes of the present, listening for a living Word of promise. It does more than simply retell the story of "Blind Bartimaeus" in "his own words." It allows Bartimaeus to speak to the congregation about the blindness he sees in the present-day community and culture—and share his story in light of this need. A sermon, in other words, doesn't limit Bartimaeus to eyewitness narration. It lets Bartimaeus preach.

   Such an effect can also be achieved by recasting Bartimaeus as an unexpected, modern-day character—especially if the congregation is adept at recognizing and responding to metaphor. Such translation can bring overlooked aspects of a familiar text into sharp relief.

- *Use the surrounding prayers and liturgy to point the congregation's attention to Christ.* One gift of theater for preaching is that it can look with clear-eyed empathy on the human condition. But people do not come to church with the single hope of seeing their human situation. They come to see Jesus. When not explicit in the sermon, Charles Bartow argues that prayers and liturgy are necessary to point the congregation to the "intervention of the person of Christ" in human life.[4] Relying on the context of worship to proclaim such grace relieves the dramatic sermon from the need to force its characters toward unrealistic, premature resolution. The sermon does not need to give "the answer." It can articulate a need that is met at the communion table—or in the prayers that follow.

- *The character portrayed should be changed in the telling.* This is hard to do but marks the difference between a preacher who is perceived as "far away" during a performance—and a preacher who is herself "converted" through the performance. If the sermon is some sort of dramatic monologue, it will most likely take the form and tone of testimony. Testimony, however, does not simply recount the past; it changes the speaker in the present. Allow the testimony you give—in the words of the character—to transform you.

- *On Sunday morning, err on the side of clarity.* Develop a sense of how much linear exposition is needed in your congregational context. In theater, it may be artful to leave intentional holes in the writing and allow the audience to fill in the gaps. But in some congregations, such gaps prove barriers to grace. Know your

4. Charles Bartow, *God's Human Speech: A Practical Theology of Proclamation* (Grand Rapids: Eerdmans, 1997) 148.

people. Your writing may be profound, resonant, and understated—but if the connection between your writing and the scriptural text is not intelligible as gospel to the young woman in the third row or the man in the back, it has not achieved its purpose.

- *Provide opportunities for response after dramatic performances.* This is difficult in many worship contexts which is why I often perform my pieces as part of Christian education settings. But it is possible. I have used a time of silent reflection on questions printed in the bulletin for this purpose, as well as continued conversation during the fellowship hour. Over time, given a congregation's comfort level, I have invited listeners to share a particular insight with the person sitting next to them in the service itself. Providing space for communal response deepens individual interpretation and can crystallize a person's experience of God through the performance. Often, these conversations leave congregations with a desire for feedback opportunities after "regular" sermons, as well.

A Note about "Small Things":

I offer the following sermon as an example of one of my attempts to use drama in a Sunday morning worship context. Unlike the other pieces in this collection, "Small Things" was performed for persons expecting a traditional sermon, and it attempts to both honor and stretch those expectations. It was performed on a day when many in the congregation would be at church twice—once for Sunday morning worship and again for the Christmas Eve service. The Scripture passage on which the piece was based was familiar to those present and woven throughout the service through music and liturgy. This particular Christmas season, many older persons in the congregation had been dealing with the death of a loved one.

The piece shows, I think, the tension between realistic dramatic representation and clear sermonic speech, but also points to the pastoral opportunity that tension provides. I do not offer it as a model but in the spirit of continuing conversation. Appropriately, given the subject of *Blessed*, it is based on Mary's Magnificat.

Small Things

Based on Mary's Magnificat, Luke 1:46–55

(Performed at Santee United Methodist Church on Christmas Eve day, 2006)

(A bird song is heard. An elderly woman enters from the back of the sanctuary wearing simple hiking clothes and a pair of binoculars. During the opening paragraph, she makes her way to the front of the church, looking for the bird.)

Did you hear it? Sounded like a vireo to me. Those little birds are making a comeback—read it in the paper. Doesn't it make you glad . . . small things alive and well? And such a pretty song. I can never seem to find them, though. I hear them, but to catch them in my sights—

(She looks through her binoculars.)

—that's a different kettle of fish. *(With an apologetic smile.)* I'm not as good at this as my husband.

I was not the birdwatcher in the family. I married into the pursuit. But after decades of traipsing through the backcountry, it grows on you. In true, San Diego style, it was our Christmas Day tradition for years. Open the gifts, a little cinnamon toast to hold you, and you're off. I protested—*(smirking)* the first dozen or so Christmases. But Peter would insist there was nothing more appropriate than birding on Christmas Day. How's that for devotion. He would quote me Emily Dickinson: "'Hope is a thing with

69

feathers'—and Christmas is about hope. It's about the importance of small things."

I suppose he was right about that. We read the Mag-
nifcat in service Sunday. You know it? The lowly lifted up
. . . the powerful brought down. Small girl, small stable,
small baby. *(With a smile.)* Small things.

(Looking a bit chagrined at talking on.) I need to sit.
You are very kind to let me go on. Would you like some
almonds?

*(She pulls some from her pocket and offers them to a
congregation member.)*

It's been a long December. First one without Peter.
Today is my first solo Christmas Day, bird-watching expe-
dition. *(Pause.)* So many firsts this year.

*(She settles herself, a bit stiffly, up-center on a rock cov-
ered with fallen leaves.)*

I used to love the wind up to Christmas. We didn't
have children, but I always bought one of those chocolate
Advent calendars . . . *(with a smile)* sometimes two. Waiting
was sweet.

Time has *crawled* by this year. Frankly, I wasn't sure
I wanted Christmas to get here or not. Part of me wanted
to be through it, past it . . . part of me dreaded it coming at
all. Some days, I wanted to be out with the birds on Christmas day—hoping to meet Peter here, I guess. Some days, I
wanted to be as far from birds as I could be.

That promise Mary's speaks of . . . where the hungry
are filled, the humble exalted . . . that's quite a bit to swallow
this year.

No Christmas music in the house. I haven't the heart
for it. I've been listening to "Quartet for the End of Time"—
Olivier Messiaen . . . rather highbrow. Peter used to like
it. Don't play it at your holiday party. *(Reflecting.)* But the
story of how that piece came about is something worth

remembering at Christmas. Or maybe I just connect it with Christmas because it's about a bird.

In 1940, as I heard it, Messiaen was a Catholic prisoner in a German war camp. Talk about time crawling. Him, I identify with this Christmas! There was a guard who knew Messiaen's music and asked him to compose something—even gave him time alone. But Messiaen couldn't write a note. Then, one day, he hears a nightingale singing outside the barbed wire. And it gets him thinking about God . . . and the end of time. And he starts writing about that coming of Christ that has nothing to do with a stable or manger, when the whole world is made new and Mary's Magnificat comes true for all of us. A piece about resurrection, really. But instead of starting with a trumpet blast, he starts it with notes that sound like a nightingale—like a bird singing in the field.

He performed the piece with three other prisoners on an old broken piano the guards scrounged up, just after Christmas 1941—and everyone was there. The guards came; the prisoners came. Some say the sick were brought in on stretchers. Enemies side-by-side, listening to hope.

And all from a nightingale. There it is again . . . the irreplaceable necessity of small things.

There are so many small things about Peter that I miss. The smell of his soap. His garden peppers. His eyeglasses on our bedside table. That's why this Christmas can't be about a starry night and a manger and sweetness and memory. I need it to be more than that.

I need it to be about a God who refuses to leave us alone—who broke into time then and who will break into time again. A God who breaks in now—because I miss the hand I used to hold . . . through small things, those irreplaceably necessary things that make all the difference in the world. Like bird song or the grace of friendly strangers on a trail. Small things . . . but big enough to usher in the promise of resurrection on Christmas morning. Big enough to fill the hungry and . . .

(She startles and stands as she sees a bird.)

There it was . . . I saw it. Did you see it? It's been sitting there the whole time.

(She can't quite believe she got a look at it.)

I saw it. Such a small thing. But . . . *(as a quiet joy dawns)* so beautiful.